Anglo-Saxon and Viking Britain

Alex Woolf

W

FRANKLIN WATTS
LONDON•SYDNEY

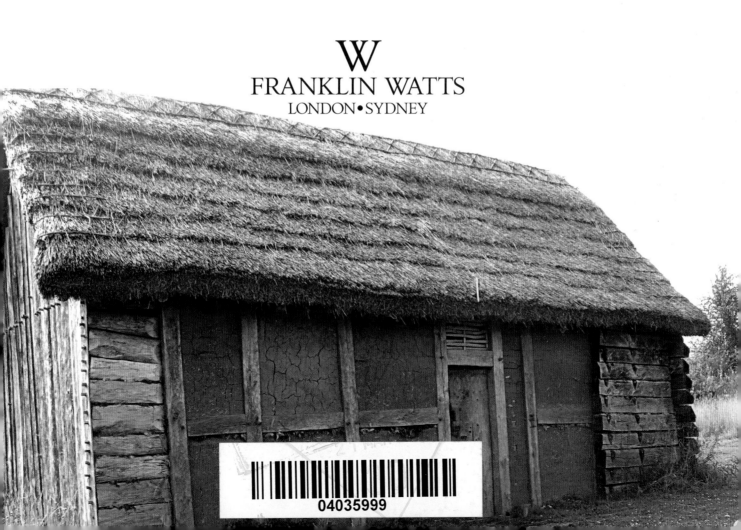

This edition 2012

First published in 2006 by
Franklin Watts
338 Euston Road
London NW1 3BH

Franklin Watts Australia
Hachette Children's Books
Level 17/207 Kent Street
Sydney NSW 2000

A CIP catalogue record for this book is
available from the British Library.

Dewey classification: 720.9

ISBN: 978 1 4451 0923 7

Printed in China

Planning and production by
Discovery Books Limited
Editor: Helen Dwyer
Design: Simon Borrough
Picture Research: Rachel Tisdale

CONTENTS

INVADERS AND SETTLERS

When the Romans left Britain in 410 CE, the country again became a target for invaders, including a group of tribes from Northern Europe – the Angles, Saxons and Jutes.

Anglo-Saxon kingdoms

By the end of the sixth century, these peoples, today known as the Anglo-Saxons, occupied almost all of southern and eastern Britain. The Anglo-Saxons established many different kingdoms and by the eighth century, there were seven main kingdoms – East Anglia, Essex, Kent, Mercia, Northumbria, Sussex and Wessex.

Arrival of the Vikings

In the late eighth century, a Scandinavian seafaring people known as the Vikings began raiding villages on the British coast. The Vikings settled in the ninth century, gradually taking control until only Wessex, ruled by Alfred the Great, remained as an independent kingdom. Alfred fought back, and in the tenth century his descendents defeated the Vikings and absorbed some Viking territory into their new kingdom, known as England (land of the Angles). The Vikings remained in control of northern and eastern England, an area known as the Danelaw.

The left-hand part of this building is an Anglo-Saxon chapel, known as Odda's Chapel. It was built in the eleventh century in the grounds of a royal house in Gloucestershire. The window's rounded top is typical of the Anglo-Saxons. A few hundred years later, in medieval times, the farmhouse on the right of the photo was built onto the chapel.

Simple buildings

The Anglo-Saxons and Vikings built many towns, houses, churches and halls in Britain. Where possible, they adapted existing Roman towns and buildings to their own needs. But the new settlers did not build like the Romans had done. Instead they brought much simpler building techniques and less grand styles of architecture from their native lands. Today only a few stone churches and the foundations of stone houses remain from Anglo-Saxon and Viking times.

This doorway is all that remains of an Anglo-Saxon church in Lewes, East Sussex. It now forms part of the wall of a nineteenth-century church.

The modern place name of Yarpole (below) comes from the Anglo-Saxon term gear-pol, meaning 'pool formed by a dam for catching fish'.

PLACE NAMES

One way of identifying Anglo-Saxon and Viking settlements is through place names. Place names ending in 'ton' (Anglo-Saxon for 'town') are a clue that Anglo-Saxons lived there. Any place name ending in 'by' was usually a Viking settlement. 'By' means 'village' in the Viking language, Old Norse.

Melmerby (above) comes from the Viking words Mael-muire-by, meaning 'St Mary's servant's village'. Wath was a Viking word meaning 'ford'.

Very few Anglo-Saxon and Viking buildings have survived because most were made from materials that have rotted away, such as wood and mud. So how do we know what buildings from this time were like? Quite a lot can be learned from the evidence in the ground.

Post-holes

Archaeologists examine post-holes – holes dug in the ground to support wooden posts – to identify structures. A typical Anglo-Saxon or Viking building would have large corner post-holes and smaller post-holes where supporting posts stood. Inside these post-holes are patches of stained soil. These are the remains of wood that has rotted away. In some post-holes, archaeologists find small pieces of pottery and stones, which were used as packing around the posts to stop them moving around in the holes.

Archaeologists excavating an Anglo-Saxon house at Thwing in the East Riding of Yorkshire. By examining the material found in post-holes, they learn about the structure and when it was built.

This excavation of an Anglo-Saxon building in Buckinghamshire has revealed that horizontal beams were placed in trenches and then wall posts were fixed to the beams (see page 15).

Doorways and hearths

Doorways are identifiable because the stone is worn down deeper than the rest of the floor. A blackened area on a clay floor, surrounded by bricks, is evidence that a hearth (fireplace) was there.

At Coppergate in York, archaeologists have excavated this stone-lined doorway to a late tenth-century Viking building.

Evidence from fire

Often the whole floor area is blackened, indicating that the building was burned down – either by accident or on purpose. Sometimes archaeologists find evidence of rebuilding above a layer of burned earth.

Carbon dating

Occasionally, archaeologists are fortunate enough to find fragments of charred (partly burned) wood that survived the fire. Wood can be dated, using a method called carbon dating, so we can find out the approximate year the fire was lit.

THE OLDEST WOODEN CHURCH IN THE WORLD

St Andrew's at Greensted-juxta-Ongar in Essex was founded in about 850 CE, making it the world's oldest surviving wooden church. The walls are built of oak logs, split in half and arranged vertically. The logs are fixed together using tongue-and-groove joints, without the use of nails. The nave is just nine metres long. The original church had no windows, and was illuminated only by candlelight. Today the wooden Saxon church is set inside a modern brick exterior.

HOUSES

There were two main types of Anglo-Saxon and Viking house – pit dwellings and framed buildings. Both types were rectangular in shape. Anglo-Saxon and Viking homes varied greatly in size, from small, single-room huts, just 3 by 3.5 metres, to vast halls of up to 22 by 80 metres.

At West Stow in Suffolk, experts have reconstructed an early Anglo-Saxon village. The houses shown here are framed buildings.

Methods and materials

Transporting heavy building materials was difficult for the Anglo-Saxons and Vikings, so people generally used locally available timber, from near the building site. Their favourite timber was oak, because it is hard. Trees were selected, felled and then cut into smaller sections before being shaped with an axe. The joints were pinned with wooden pegs called trenails.

This close-up of a reconstructed Anglo-Saxon house at the Bishops Wood Centre near Worcester shows the trenails (wooden pegs) that were driven into bored holes to form a secure joint between two beams. Iron was very expensive in Anglo-Saxon times, which is why trenails were made of wood.

Roofs

Roofs were either thatched with reed or straw, or sometimes shingled with overlapping wooden tiles nailed to the roof frame. There were no chimneys, and smoke escaped through openings high up in the gable.

Wattle and daub buildings (see panel, right) usually had extra-wide roofs so that the eaves gave good shelter from the rain. Archaeologists know this because the water flowing off the roof formed a channel in the ground, known as the eavesdrip.

Windows

Most houses had no windows, and were probably dark and smelly places. Those that did have windows may have had vellum stretched over them to let some light in and keep draughts out. In later times, some of the wealthier homes may have had windows with glass.

WATTLE AND DAUB

Panels of thin wooden sticks interwoven with flexible shoots or twigs (wattle) were placed between rows of wooden posts. Then they were covered with a mixture of mud, straw and manure (daub), and smoothed to give an even finish. Wattle and daub walls were easy to build and maintain and provided good insulation, but would quickly deteriorate if exposed to rain or damp.

A close-up of the roof of a reconstructed Anglo-Saxon hall at the Bishops Wood Centre. Materials used for thatching included water reed, wheat reed and long straw. The thatching material was secured to the roof by hazel or willow sticks twisted in the middle to form a staple.

INSIDE THE HOME

The interiors of Anglo-Saxon and Viking dwellings were very simple. Floors would have been packed earth or wood. Some larger houses may have had raised wooden floors with steps leading up to the entrance. Floors were often strewn with straw and sweet-smelling herbs.

Doors and walls

Doors had iron or wooden hinges and closed with a latch. Some doors also had locks. Most houses did not have internal walls, and those that did were usually made of wattle and daub.

Heating and lighting

Light would come from candles or lamps and from a central fire built on a raised clay hearth. Hearths were generally rectangular and often had a frame of wood or stone. A few houses may also have had a clay bread oven.

Anglo-Saxon doors were made of large planks of timber, usually oak. Doors and frames were usually very plain, with few decorations, as in this reconstruction at the Bishops Wood Centre.

As can be seen in this reconstruction from West Stow in Suffolk, Anglo-Saxon houses had few items of furniture. The fire in the centre was used for both heating and cooking. The willow panels on the windows would have let some light in, but they could not have kept out the draughts.

Furniture and furnishings

Homes contained very little furniture. There were chests, a table and some stools. Only the wealthiest people sat on chairs. Some Viking halls had raised wooden earth-filled benches down each side of the hall – for seating during the day and sleeping on at night. Wealthier people may have had a wooden bed with a straw-filled mattress, screened off from the main hall by a curtain.

No Anglo-Saxon furniture survives, but there are traces of built-in benches and storage chests at the sites of small dwellings. Cloth hangings or skins around the walls kept draughts out. War and hunting trophies adorned the walls of great halls.

This reconstruction of the interior of a typical Anglo-Saxon house is at Bede's World in Jarrow. It has simple, crudely made benches, an earthen floor, and no internal walls to divide it into smaller rooms.

VIKING LONGHOUSES

Country-dwelling Vikings built themselves long, narrow dwellings called longhouses. Sometimes these houses would have just one room, with posts rather than interior walls supporting the roof. In other cases, they had family rooms at one end and stables for horses and cattle at the other. In places where wood was not plentiful, longhouses had roofs made of turf.

The remains of two Viking longhouses on the Isle of Man (below). The nearer longhouse was used as living quarters for a farmer and his family. It had curved walls made of turf with the ends made of timber. There were no internal walls. The other longhouse was used for farm animals. The circle at the back of the picture is a Celtic stone roundhouse from an earlier period.

PIT DWELLINGS

Pit dwellings had a lowered floor or pit, sunk into the earth. Remains of these have been found in places such as York, Dorchester in Oxfordshire, Lakenheath in Suffolk and Maxey in Northamptonshire.

Living and storage space

Why did people choose to live in sunken houses? One reason may have been for protection from the weather. However, there's also plenty of evidence to suggest that they covered the pits with wooden floors and used the underfloor space for storage. These floors have long since disappeared, but the remains of hearths indicate that they may have fallen through a floor when it rotted away. Also, the pit floors are not damaged in ways to suggest that people walked around on them.

This reconstruction in the grounds of Bentley House, Sussex, is an example of the simplest type of pit dwelling. It has a wooden-shingled roof built directly onto the ground, enclosing a pit edged with wooden planks.

How were they constructed?

The simplest types of pit dwelling were workshops and were no more than a pit enclosed by a roof. Those used as houses had low walls. These walls were probably built from earth extracted when the pit was dug out, and strengthened with twigs. The pit was usually around 0.5 to 1 metre deep. The sides and floor of the pit were often lined with wooden planks or wattle, as in the house excavated in York, pictured below.

This deep Viking pit dwelling was excavated at Coppergate in York. Its walls are lined with sticks (wattle) that were woven around wooden posts.

The walls surrounded the pit. Wooden posts at either end supported a central roof beam. The roof rafters extended to the ground on either side, supported by the tops of the low walls. The main living area was in the central section, with its hearth.

Cellared buildings

After 950 CE, another type of pit dwelling appeared, with floors up to 2.5 metres below ground level, accessed by a set of steps. With no sign of a hearth, it is likely that these cellared buildings were used as warehouses or workshops.

Anglo-Saxon and Viking roofs had evenly spaced rafters that joined the roof to the walls. The tile or thatch was supported by thin wooden slats called battens.

FRAMED BUILDINGS

Framed buildings had much higher walls than pit dwellings. They also tended to be much larger than pit dwellings, and some even had a second storey. They were strong because a large number of posts were set into the ground, supporting the timber frame.

Posts, beams and buttresses

These posts could be set as deep as 2.4 metres on larger buildings. Upright posts were placed at each corner. Other timber posts were placed between these at regular intervals. Horizontal beams were placed between the vertical posts and between the side walls at the same height as the eaves to give the structure strength. The roofs of larger structures were supported by a row of posts inside the building. Some had wooden buttresses around the outside for added support.

In this reconstruction of an Anglo-Saxon framed building at the Bishops Wood Centre in Worcestershire the walls are constructed partly of wattle and daub and partly of horizontal wooden planks.

Walls, floors and hearths

The walls were constructed with wattle and daub, planks or both. The planks either overlapped horizontally or were set vertically. Draughts were kept out with sheep's wool or dried grass. The floors were sometimes just packed earth, but could also be planked, cobbled or covered in slaked lime. There was usually a raised hearth in the centre of the building.

The door of a reconstructed timber-framed building at the Bishops Wood Centre. The door and the surrounding frame were built from freshly felled oak trees, carved with axes into square beams.

The gaps between the horizontal planks on timber-framed buildings were often stuffed with sheep's wool in order to keep out the draughts.

Different styles

In parts of Hampshire examples of a type of framed building called a 'cruck' building have been found, dating from the seventh century. In this style of building, pairs of timber posts extend from ground level, curving inwards to meet at the central roof beam.

Between the eight and tenth centuries, the foundations of framed buildings changed with the introduction of the sill beam – a horizontal beam either placed on the ground surface or set in a trench. Wall posts were then fixed to this rather than being placed directly into the ground. By the tenth century, many of the grander houses were built in stone.

This reconstructed workshop at West Stow in Suffolk has an oak frame with an infill of wattle and clay.

15

STONE BUILDINGS

For 200 years after the departure of the Romans, the tradition of building in stone all but vanished from Britain. Both Anglo-Saxons and Vikings preferred to build even their largest buildings out of wood. Stone was occasionally used in the walls of buildings in parts of the country where timber was scarce, such as in the Outer Hebrides, Orkney and Shetland.

Churches and great halls

The spread of Christianity encouraged the use of stone as a material for building churches. The first churches were built in the early 600s, but it was not until the ninth or tenth centuries, that stone-built, non-religious buildings began reappearing across Britain. These were the great halls of the Viking and Anglo-Saxon nobility.

Here are two examples of typical Anglo-Saxon stonework – a herringbone pattern on the wall of Wigmore church, Herefordshire (left) and pilasters (vertical strips) on the walls of Stanton Lacy church, Shropshire (right).

Construction

Stone was sometimes transported by river or by sea, but rarely over land. Stone cargoes have been found in numerous Viking shipwrecks. In many cases, stones from old Roman buildings were reused. The stone was worked into shape by masons using a hammer or mallet and a chisel.

These elaborately carved stone monuments with curved sides and top are called hogbacks. They were created by Vikings and date from the tenth to the twelfth centuries. Many have been found in northern England and Scotland. Hogbacks may have had religious significance.

Some masons were in charge of erecting buildings, while others were responsible for decorating them. Carved windows, door surrounds, pillars and friezes were usually made from easily worked sandstone or limestone. The carvings were often painted. Traces of paint have been found in the nooks and crannies of many carvings.

An Anglo-Saxon sundial on St Gregory's Minster at Kirkdale in North Yorkshire. The Anglo-Saxons created the first sundials in Britain. They were often carved into the stonework on the south-facing walls of churches.

Ornamental stonework

The later Anglo-Saxons used stone for a number of structures and monuments, including sundials, crosses, seats, fonts and gravestones, many of which survive at the sites of churches. The crosses were often elaborately carved and painted in colours such as black, blue, red, brown, orange and white. Vikings also built stone crosses, often with pagan symbols on one side and Christian symbols on the other – perhaps to make sure that no god was left out!

CHURCHES

The Christian Church grew gradually in Britain from its introduction in the third century to become the most widely-followed religion by the mid-seventh century. The earliest Christians built carved stone crosses to mark their places of worship. Later, churches were built on these sites.

Two traditions

When they invaded Britain, the pagan Anglo-Saxons drove many Christian Britons west to northern England, Wales, Cornwall and Ireland, where a Celtic form of Christianity grew. Then, after 600 CE, a more Romanised tradition of Christianity gradually took hold among the Anglo-Saxons. These two distinct forms of Christianity are reflected in the architecture of the churches that began to appear from the 650s.

Southern Britain's churches followed the Roman model. These had chambers to each side of the nave, with a semicircular projecting chancel at the east end. Northern churches followed the Celtic model. They were simpler in design, with no side chambers and rectangular chancels. The interiors were decorated with colourful wall paintings.

The church of St Peter on the Wall at Bradwell-on-Sea in Essex (above) is the oldest stone church in Britain of which so much remains. It was built between 654 and 660 CE, using materials from a nearby Roman fort, including red roof tiles still visible in its walls.

The tiny crypt (a room under a church, often used for burials) of Ripon Abbey in North Yorkshire (left) is all that remains of a church built on this site in 672 CE. It is the oldest complete Anglo-Saxon crypt.

Structure

Large Anglo-Saxon churches and monasteries were rebuilt by the Normans from the eleventh century onwards. Surviving churches are small, with simple doors and windows and few decorative elements compared to the grander Norman style. Windows were usually deep-set vertical slits with rounded tops. Larger window openings were often supported by short, plain stone pillars.

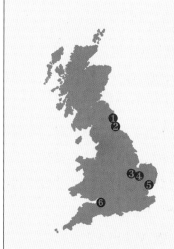

All Saints' Church in Brixworth, Northamptonshire, was built around 680 CE and is the largest seventh-century structure to have survived in Britain. It is famous for its tiled arches. The tower was later made taller, and the spire was added in the 14th century.

SEE FOR YOURSELF
Examples of Celtic-style churches include the monastic buildings at Monkwearmouth and Jarrow, Tyne and Wear (1) and the church at Escomb, County Durham (2). Several well-preserved examples survive of Roman-style Anglo-Saxon churches, including Brixworth (3) and Earls Barton (4), both in Northamptonshire, Bradwell-on-Sea in Essex (5) and Bradford-on-Avon in Wiltshire (6).

Church towers

The most prominent feature of many of today's parish churches – their tower – is also often the oldest surviving part. The Anglo-Saxons originally built these towers as defensive structures. They provided useful lookout points for villagers to give early warning of attacks.

The tower of the tenth-century Anglo-Saxon church at Bosham in West Sussex. The builders of this church used the typical Anglo-Saxon style of alternating horizontal and vertical stones at the corners of the tower.

GREAT HALLS

Anglo-Saxon nobles built themselves great halls at the centres of their estates where they and their household lived, ate and slept. These were surrounded by smaller buildings – storehouses, guest houses, workshops, stables, servants' houses, a bake-house and a chapel – all enclosed by a defensive wall called a stockade.

Royal palaces

The most important archaeological excavations have been the royal palace at Yeavering and at King Alfred's royal estate at Cheddar. Alfred's great hall was 24 metres long by 6 metres at its widest. Its side walls were curved so that the width across the centre was greater than at either end. The post-holes reveal a timber-framed construction with a row of inner posts suggesting there may have been a second storey.

YEAVERING ROYAL PALACE

The remains of the early-seventh century palace of King Edwin can be seen at Yeavering, Northumberland. Excavation has revealed two great halls, with one over 20 metres long. There was also a building containing semi-circular banked seating for 300 people. This may have been used as a meeting chamber, or for preaching.

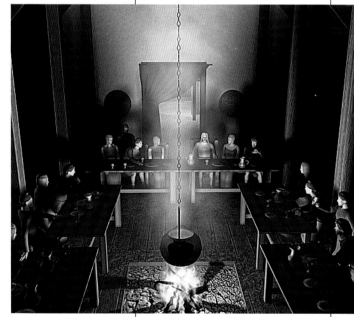

These are artists' reconstructions of the site of the royal palace at Yeavering (left) and of the interior of one of the halls during a feast (right).

The structure of a great hall

At first, great halls were all timber-framed, but later, they were built from stone. Usually rectangular in shape, their entrances were in the middle of the longer sides. Great halls were always roofed in timber. The roofs were supported by two rows of wooden columns running the length of the building.

Inside the great hall

The hall was divided into two rooms. The smaller room was probably a bedroom for the noble and his family. The main room was the feasting hall, where the noble would gather with his soldiers to eat and relax. A large central hearth provided heat and light. There may also have been flaming torches on the walls, along with decorative wall hangings. The floor was probably covered with rushes or straw.

A reconstruction by the re-enactment society Regia Anglorum of an Anglo-Saxon great hall near Canterbury in Kent. It is constructed from oak using many of the tools and techniques of the period.

When Anglo-Saxon and Viking invaders began to settle they looked around for good farmland. Some took over existing farms, while others cleared forests to grow their crops and make pasture for their sheep and cattle.

The farms consisted of several buildings. The farmer and his family lived, ate and slept in the largest building. Smaller buildings included a byre (for cattle), a stable, a barn for threshing and storing corn, a dairy and a workshop. The main building was rectangular, with an open-plan interior and a sloped thatched roof. The workshop, or smithy, contained the blacksmith's forge.

Farm to village

The first Anglo-Saxon settlements were groups of three or four family farms encircled by a protective fence. In time, these developed into villages. Most villages contained a large hall belonging to the local leader, where villagers could meet. As the village grew, the defences were improved to include an earth bank and ditch with defended gates. The earth bank was topped by a timber fence made from pointed stakes.

HURDLES

Farmers made wattle panels called hurdles (like the modern replicas in the picture) by interweaving thin sticks with flexible willow twigs. They used these for fencing, to act as screens around outdoor toilets, and to make paths across boggy ground. Hurdles are still used on farms today as portable fences to enclose sheep and other animals. The word, based on the Old English *hyrdel*, meaning temporary fence, is now used to describe the obstacles in a modern athletics race.

An aerial view of the Viking settlement at Jarlshof in Shetland, which was lived in for 400 years.

A Viking farm

At Jarlshof in Shetland, a Viking farm from the ninth century has been excavated. The main farmhouse (shown right) was a rectangular building with two doorways on opposite sides. Inside the farmhouse were two rooms, a long hall and a smaller kitchen. A fire burned in the centre of the hall and an oven was

built into the end wall. Central timber posts supported the roof, which was probably covered with turf. The farmer and his family sat and slept on raised wooden platforms that ran the length of the walls. Other buildings at Jarlshof included a byre, a smithy and a heated building that may have been used for drying grain, or possibly as a sauna (steam bath).

The farmhouse at Jarlshof originally had a byre (cattle shelter) at one end and the family living quarters at the other. Later the cattle were moved to a separate outhouse.

The Viking settlement on the island of Birsay in Orkney contains the remains pictured below that have been identified as a possible sauna and bathhouse.

FORTIFIED TOWNS

To defend the Anglo-Saxon kingdom of Wessex from the Vikings, Alfred the Great built a series of fortified towns, called burhs, manned by soldiers and offering shelter to local people in time of attack. The burhs were located in many parts of southern England, concentrated mainly along the coast and borders of Alfred's lands. No settlement was more than 32 kilometres from a burh.

Re-using Roman towns

The streets of these burhs were laid out in a grid pattern, similar to Roman towns. In fact some were actually built on old Roman towns and there were good reasons for this. Roman towns had good communication links. They also had earthwork defences already in place, which could easily be repaired and strengthened. The original Roman main street was often reused, as at Chichester (Sussex) and Winchester (Hampshire). The Anglo-Saxons often used Roman streets as foundations for their houses, with new streets running alongside.

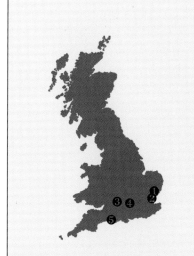

SEE FOR YOURSELF
Remnants of burh defensive fortifications can still be seen in the following towns.
1 Witham, Essex
2 Maldon, Essex
3 Cricklade, Wiltshire
4 Wallingford, Oxfordshire
5 Wareham, Dorset

Part of the wall that provided the main defence for Anglo-Saxon Hereford. A wooden wall known as a revetment, reconstructed here (see background), helped to increase the overall height of the defensive barrier.

Coastal defences

Other burhs were built on the sites of pre-Roman coastal forts, such as at Lydford (Devon), Christchurch (Hampshire), Burpham and Lewes (both Sussex). These forts had been raised on steep-sided points of land that jutted into the sea. Earthwork ramparts were added to the natural defences to make the burhs even more secure against Viking raiders. At Lydford, a 12-metre-wide bank surrounded the town. Excavations have shown that the interior of the bank was strengthened by a line of upright timbers, which may have supported fighting platforms.

Portchester Castle in Hampshire was originally a Roman fortress. The Anglo-Saxons made use of the old Roman defences when they turned it into a fortified burh.

New towns

A third type of burh was built on completely new sites. Examples include Wallingford (Oxfordshire), Wareham (Dorset) and Wilton (Wiltshire). Here, new defences were built, consisting of a surrounding earth rampart faced with wood or stone and fronted by a deep ditch.

Saxon street plans

Many burhs still survive as modern towns, and in Winchester, Cricklade (Wiltshire), Chichester and Wallingford, the modern streets follow the original Anglo-Saxon street plan.

Winchester became the most important burh in the kingdom of Wessex, and its cathedral was the burial place of Alfred the Great. The present-day cathedral, shown here, is Norman and dates from 1079. The Anglo-Saxon structure was situated just to the north.

JORVIK – A VIKING TOWN

In 866 CE the Anglo-Saxon town of Eoforwic (modern-day York) was captured by the Vikings, who renamed it Jorvik. Under the Vikings, Jorvik doubled in size and grew into Britain's largest trading city.

Jorvik expands

The Vikings laid out new streets and built houses and workshops of wood and wattle and daub with thatched roofs. They lengthened the quayside and repaired the old Roman walls.

Excavations in Coppergate

One area, Coppergate, is the site of the largest Viking excavation in Britain. Archaeologists studying this site have made a detailed study of the remains of four plots. The oldest houses on this site (those found deepest under the soil) were built in the early tenth century. The long narrow properties were divided by hurdle fencing.

PAST TO PRESENT

Modern York follows the same street plan as originally laid down by the Vikings. Clues to its heritage can be found in the street names, especially those ending in 'gate' (Old Norse *gata*, meaning 'street'): Skeldergate (shieldmakers' street), Hungate (dogs' street) and Coppergate (coopers', or woodworkers' street).

Archaeologists at work on the site of a tenth-century wattle-and-daub building in Coppergate. The remains of a hearth can be seen in the foreground. Excavations at Coppergate have uncovered a great deal of evidence about Viking houses, workshops and other buildings.

Early houses

These houses were, on average, 4.5 metres wide and around 7 metres long, with their gables facing the street. They were constructed of wattle and daub on a timber framework, and must have been fairly flimsy because the archaeological evidence shows they were rebuilt a number of times.

Later houses

Then, in the 950s, all four houses were rebuilt much more sturdily as pit dwellings with strong foundation posts, walls of horizontal oak planks and roofs of wood shingles. These were the first well-preserved Viking timber buildings ever found in Britain (below). Jewellery and wooden objects found there indicate that these buildings doubled as houses and shops.

In this reconstruction of a street scene from Viking Jorvik (above) a stallholder sells his wares.

The remains of vertical foundation posts and walls constructed of horizontal planks have survived from a tenth-century pit dwelling in Coppergate.

PAST TO PRESENT

One of the rebuilt York houses was given a double-layered wall, filled with a mesh of willow twigs and brushwood. This was very similar to a type of cavity wall insulation known as wood wool, used in Scandinavia until the nineteenth century.

BURIAL SITES

The Anglo-Saxons and Vikings believed in life after death. In order to make their journey to the next world easier, people were buried with some of their most precious possessions. Several burial sites have been found near Anglo-Saxon and Viking settlements. Chieftains and kings were given very elaborate burials.

Sutton Hoo

An extraordinary Anglo-Saxon burial site was discovered at Sutton Hoo in Suffolk in 1939. Beneath a mound of earth, archaeologists found a large treasure ship, nearly 30 metres long. The ship's timbers had rotted away, but its shape was clear.

Inside the ship, archaeologists found a specially built burial chamber. Many valuable objects were found, including weapons and armour and a lyre (a stringed musical instrument) – but no body. Perhaps the site was a memorial rather than a grave – but whose memorial was it? The most likely candidate is Redwald, an East Anglian king who died in about 627 CE.

One of several low grassy mounds that make up the Anglo-Saxon burial site of Sutton Hoo. Further excavation work in the 1960s and 1970s revealed the site to contain a number of burials, many of them of important, possibly royal, people.

28

TAPLOW MOUND

Taplow Mound in Buckinghamshire dates from 620 CE and was the richest Anglo-Saxon burial until the discovery of Sutton Hoo. Finds include drinking horns, a harp and a bronze bowl from Egypt. The mound was erected in the grounds of a now-demolished church.

A replica of a richly decorated Anglo-Saxon helmet found at Sutton Hoo in Suffolk.

A grave at the Anglo-Saxon burial site at RAF Lakenheath in Suffolk containing the remains of a man and his horse. The site dates from the fifth to seventh centuries, and probably served a nearby settlement.

Viking burials

Vikings believed that they could travel to the afterlife by boat, and the bodies of noble Vikings were often placed, along with their possessions, in ships which were then buried under huge mounds or burned. One such ship grave can be seen at Balladoole, Isle of Man (below). Sometimes Vikings were buried in a ring of stones laid out in the shape of a boat.

SEE FOR YOURSELF

Viking burial sites can be found at Scar on Orkney (1), Balladoole, Isle of Man (2) and Barrow in Cumbria (3). Anglo-Saxon burial sites include Eriswell (pictured above) at RAF Lakenheath, Suffolk (4), Sutton Hoo, Suffolk (5) and Prittlewell in Essex (6).

The Viking ship-shaped grave at Balladoole on the Isle of Man. The site, which was excavated in 1974, contained an 11-metre-long Viking ship.

29

TIMELINE

CE 400s	Angles, Saxons and Jutes arrive and settle in Britain.
597	St Augustine founds a monastery at Canterbury.
c.624	Sutton Hoo ship burial of a Saxon king.
635	Lindisfarne monastery established.
772–775	King Offa of Mercia builds a dyke from north Wales to the River Severn to keep out the Welsh.
789–795	First Viking attacks on Britain.
c.800	Vikings settle in Shetland and Orkney.
865–867	Great Viking Army from Denmark invades England. Danes capture York and make it their capital.
878	King Alfred of Wessex makes a treaty with the Vikings, dividing England into Anglo-Saxon England and the Viking Danelaw.
900–937	Anglo-Saxons reconquer most of the Danelaw.
980	New Viking raids on England.
1013–1042	Vikings rule England.
1042–1066	Anglo-Saxons rule England.
1066	Normans conquer England.
1266	Vikings lose control of lands in Scotland but keep islands of Orkney and Shetland.
1469	Orkney and Shetland become part of Scotland. End of Viking rule in Britain.

GLOSSARY

buttress a solid structure that is built against a wall to support it.

cavity wall insulation a way of preventing the loss of heat from a house by filling the hollow spaces within a wall with material.

Celtic relating to the Celts, a people who lived in Britain since before the Roman conquest.

chancel the area of a church near the altar.

eaves the parts of the roof that project beyond the walls that support them.

font a large container in a church for the water used in baptisms.

forge a furnace used to heat metal to a very high temperature.

frieze a horizontal band of decoration found on the walls of buildings such as churches.

gable the triangle formed by the angles of a pitched roof.

mason someone who makes things out of stone.

nave the long central hall of a church.

Normans a Viking people based in northern France, who conquered England in 1066.

pagan a follower of an ancient religion who worships many gods.

post-hole a hole that is dug to receive an upright timber for a building.

rampart a defensive fortification made of an earth embankment often topped by a low wall.

shingles small wooden tiles.

slaked lime a substance made by adding water to quicklime and used to make plaster or mortar.

smithy the place where a blacksmith works.

sundial an instrument that shows the time of day by the position of the sun's shadow cast by a fixed arm on a plate.

tongue-and-groove joints joints between wooden boards in which a thin, protruding section (a tongue) runs along the edge of one board and fits into a long groove in the other.

vellum the skin of a calf, lamb or young goat.

PLACES TO VISIT

Bede's World, Jarrow
www.bedesworld.co.uk
Site of the Anglo-Saxon monastery of St Paul, where the monk and historian Bede lived and worked 1,300 years ago. You can visit the interactive Age of Bede exhibition as well as the rare breeds of animals and recreated timber buildings on Gyrwe, the Anglo-Saxon demonstration farm.

Bishops Wood Centre, Worcestershire
www.bishopswoodcentre.org.uk
(select 'Buildings' under 'Direct Links')
This environmental education centre for Worcestershire schools contains a reconstructed Anglo-Saxon hall made by volunteers, including school groups, with tools the Anglo-Saxons would have used. The frame is made of green oak and the walls are clad with oak boards and wattle and daub.

British Museum, London
www.britishmuseum.org/
Visit the museum or use their website to find out more about the Sutton Hoo artefacts and other objects dating from the same era. Use the Young Explorer part of the website to investigate Anglo-Saxon England. Some Anglo-Saxon and Viking objects were featured in the British Museum/BBC History of the World series. Check them out at: www.bbc.co.uk/ahistoryoftheworld/about/british-museum-objects/

Brixworth Church, Northamptonshire
www.britannia.com/church/saxchurch/brixworth1.html
The best preserved Anglo-Saxon building in Britain. All Saints' Church was probably built around 680 CE. It is famous for its tiled arches and its ring crypt.

Jarlshof, Sumburgh Head, Shetland
www.shetland-heritage.co.uk/jarlshof
Visit Jarlshof to see the remains of a Viking settlement that spanned more than 400 years. There are the remains of a Viking longhouse, with a byre at one end and the family area at the other, with outhouses for the animals attached to the main house.

Jorvik Viking Centre, York
www.jorvik-viking-centre.co.uk
Discover what life was really like more than 1,000 years ago. See over 800 items uncovered in York and journey through a reconstruction of York's Viking-age streets.

Museum of London
www.museumoflondon.org.uk (type 'Saxon' in 'Search')
Visit the Medieval London gallery, which explores the city's history from the end of Roman times to the mid-16th century.

Sutton Hoo, Woodbridge, Suffolk
www.nationaltrust.org.uk/suttonhoo/
An Anglo-Saxon royal burial site where royal treasures were discovered in a huge ship grave. The exhibition presents finds from the burial.

West Stow Anglo-Saxon Village, Suffolk
www.stedmundsbury.gov.uk/weststow/
West Stow, the early Anglo-Saxon village, has been carefully reconstructed where it was excavated. Visitors can go into the houses and imagine living in early Anglo-Saxon times. In the Anglo-Saxon Centre, objects from the original village are displayed, telling the story of this settlement and the people who lived here.

INDEX